MW01699140

Specific Skill Series
for Reading

Sequencing

Sixth Edition

Columbus, OH

The McGraw·Hill Companies

Cover: © Royalty-Free/Corbis

SRAonline.com

SRA

Printed in the United States of America.

Send all inquiries to:
SRA/McGraw-Hill
4400 Easton Commons
Columbus, OH 43219

ISBN 0-07-604037-2

3 4 5 6 7 8 9 BCH 13 12 11 10 09 08 07

TO THE TEACHER

PURPOSE:

SEQUENCING helps develop the important ability to determine time relationships—the order in which things happen. Proficiency in this often taken-for-granted skill is necessary in all kinds of academic and nonacademic reading, from narration to process explanation.

FOR WHOM:

The skill of **SEQUENCING** is developed through a series of books spanning ten levels (Picture, Preparatory, A, B, C, D, E, F, G, H). The Picture Level is for students who have not acquired a basic sight vocabulary. The Preparatory Level is for students who have a basic sight vocabulary but are not yet ready for the first-grade-level book. Books A through H are appropriate for students who can read on levels one through eight, respectively.

THE NEW EDITION:

SEQUENCING has been designed to help improve students' skills in identifying the sequence of events within a reading selection. In this series, the variety of questions helps develop students' understanding of multiple ways of expressing time relationships. Questions are text-dependent rather than picture-dependent.

SESSIONS:

Short practice sessions are the most effective. It is desirable to have a practice session every day or every other day, using a few units each session.

SCORING:

Students should record their answers on the reproducible worksheets. The worksheets make scoring easier and provide uniform records of the students' work. Using worksheets also avoids consuming the exercise books.

TO THE TEACHER

It is important for students to know how well they are doing. For this reason, units should be scored as soon as they have been completed. Then a discussion can be held in which students justify their choices. (The *Language Activity Pages,* many of which are open-ended, do not lend themselves to an objective score; thus there are no answer keys for these pages.)

GENERAL INFORMATION ON *SEQUENCING:*

SEQUENCING helps develop sequence skills through three general types of questions: (1) those that focus directly on when an event happened; (2) those that focus on which of several events happened first (or last) among the events mentioned; and (3) those that focus on whether a particular event happened before, at the same time, or after another. The teacher should make clear to students that a question reading "Which happened first (last)?" means "Which happened before (after) any of the *other answer choices?"* (not "Which happened first [last] in the *entire reading selection?*").

Answering questions in **SEQUENCING** involves more than just reading for facts. Most questions require students to establish the time relationships between two separately stated ideas by utilizing time clues in the text. (In the Picture Level, students examine two pictures illustrating a sequence of events and determine which event happened first.)

SUGGESTED STEPS:

In all levels above Picture, students should read each story carefully. At the end of each statement they should try to form a picture in their minds so they will clearly understand what happened first, second, and so forth. As they read, students should look for key words that serve as sequence clues, such as *then, before, soon, finally, later, while, when,* and *now.* After finishing the story, students should review it mentally. Without looking at the story, they should be able to recall the sequence in which events occurred. If they cannot do this, they should reread the story. Students should then answer the questions on their worksheets. In answering, students may look at the story as often as necessary.

RELATED MATERIALS:

Specific Skill Series Assessment Book provides the teacher with a pretest and a posttest for each skill at each grade level. These tests will help the teacher assess the students' performance in each of the nine comprehension skills.

About This Book

In real life, things happen in a certain order. You do one thing. Then you do another thing. This is called *sequence.* Sequence is the order in which things (events) happen. Other names for *sequence* are *time order* and *1-2-3 order.*

Story events happen in a certain order too. In a story something happens. Then something else happens. Often one event causes the events that follow.

The events in a story are usually told in the order in which things happened. The paragraph below uses this order.

> Sue was fixing an old bike. She put a new chain on it. She gave the bike a fresh coat of paint. The bike looked almost new.

Sometimes events may be told out of order. Read the sentence below. Use clues to figure out the correct order of events.

> Before he got on his bike, Sam checked the tires.

Did Sam get on his bike first or check the tires first? The word *before* tells you that he checked the tires first. Words like *after, before, while, then, next, first,* and *last* are clues to the sequence of events. Another clue is the natural order of events. Could you ride your bike before you got on it?

In this book, you will read many different kinds of stories. As you read, look for clues that let you know the order in which things happened. Then answer questions about the sequence of events.

Unit 1
The Giant Pumpkin

Can you imagine a pumpkin big enough for you to sit in? Don Fleming can, because he grew it. The pumpkin weighed more than 604 pounds!

Fleming lives on a farm in Vermont. When the giant pumpkin was fully grown, he entered it in a contest. No other pumpkin was as big as Fleming's. The judges gave him the prize for the largest pumpkin of the year.

After the contest was over, Fleming sat down to think. What could he do with the giant pumpkin? The answer came to him very quickly. He would turn the pumpkin into a giant jack-o'-lantern!

To get started, Fleming asked his neighbor, Doug Small, to help. The two then set to work cutting through the tough skin of the pumpkin. They cut for several minutes. Finally they had a round hole for the jack-o'-lantern's nose. The nose, by the way, was six inches thick and the size of a watermelon!

For hours the two men worked on the pumpkin. After they cut out the nose, they got to work on the two large eyes. Then they started to make the mouth. The pumpkin weighed so much that Fleming and Small were afraid to make one large mouth. The weight of the pumpkin might have made it fall in. They cut four smaller holes for "teeth" along the bottom of the face.

After three hours of work, the face was ready. Soon people were running to see it. Kids got a big surprise. They could climb right inside Fleming's pumpkin and look out.

The only thing left to worry about was what to do with all of the soft insides of the pumpkin. Soon Fleming and his friends were hard at work. After all, it takes quite a while to make 400 pumpkin pies!

Unit 1
The Giant Pumpkin

A+

1. What happened first?
   (A) Don Fleming asked Doug Small to help.
   (B) Don Fleming decided to make a giant jack-o'-lantern.
   (C) Don Fleming entered his pumpkin in a contest.

2. What did Fleming do before he started working on the jack-o'-lantern's nose?
   (A) He asked Doug Small to help him.
   (B) Kids climbed inside the pumpkin.
   (C) Two large eyes were made.

3. When did Don decide to make pumpkin pies?
   (A) After the jack-o'-lantern was finished
   (B) Before he won the prize
   (C) When he was making the nose

4. What happened last?
   (A) Everyone took pictures of the jack-o'-lantern.
   (B) People started making pies.
   (C) Kids climbed inside the pumpkin.

Unit 2
Looking for a Legend

Fourteen-year-old Sebastian Calaway was surprised. His father had just asked him if he wanted to go to Scotland. Then he was even more surprised. His father said they were going to search for the famous Loch Ness Monster.

For more than 1,400 years, people have told stories about a strange creature. The monster is supposed to live in this Scottish lake, or "loch." No one has ever been able to prove the monster exists, but many people still believe in it.

Sebastian and his father got ready. As soon as they arrived at the lake, 20 boats set out. They quickly formed a line across the loch. They began to move slowly down the lake. First, the searchers used "fish finders" to find out what was on the bottom of the lake. Each fish finder sent out radio waves that bounced off anything below. These "echoes" showed up on a screen that looked like a television screen. This helped the group find anything unusual. Then underwater television cameras were lowered into the water. They sent back pictures of what they saw below.

For hours the boats moved from one end of the lake to the other. The equipment found fish, underwater junk, and large rocks. They found no Loch Ness Monster. Finally, toward evening, one of the boats received an unusual signal. Other boats rushed to find out what it was, but the signal disappeared.

The group kept going, day after day. They found more fish and more junk. They even found a huge tree stump that looked a bit like a monster's head. Everyone was disappointed, especially Adrian Shine, the leader of the group. Shine had spent almost 20 years searching for the Loch Ness Monster. However, he did not give up hope. Within days he and the others had made plans to try again. Maybe next time they really will find out that this beautiful lake in Scotland is home to one of the world's most famous legends.

Unit 2
Looking for a Legend

1. What happened first?

(A) Sebastian and his father went to Scotland.
(B) A boat received an unusual signal.
(C) The boats set out on the lake.

---

2. What happened before the boats lowered underwater television cameras?

(A) They used “fish finders” to find unusual objects.
(B) They decided that there was no monster in the lake.
(C) They decided to come back and try again.

---

3. When did the group get the unusual signal?

(A) Just before they ended the trip
(B) When they found a huge tree stump
(C) Toward evening of the first day

---

4. What happened last?

(A) They found a huge tree stump.
(B) They made plans for another search.
(C) Adrian Shine started searching for the monster.

Unit 3
Eggs, Eggs Everywhere

Most people have seen brightly decorated eggs—but Dorothy Crall of Irwin, Pennsylvania, probably has seen more of these eggs than anyone else. Crall has been collecting decorated eggs for many years. Today her egg collection just might be the largest one in the world.

Crall began her collection years ago. At the same time she also began coloring eggs herself. Later she began asking artists to make special eggs for her. "I hand them an egg," she says, "and ask them to do some artwork on it."

As of now, Crall has painted more than 2,500 eggs of her own. She has collected another 4,500 eggs painted by other people. Her fondest dream is to open an egg museum. In the museum she would display a variety of eggs. Some would be decorated. Some would not. The museum would show people the beautiful kinds of eggs that can be found in the world.

Some of Crall's favorite eggs are old ones. Years ago, in Russia and other countries in Eastern Europe, decorated eggs were very important. Eggs were given as gifts. They also were used as good-luck charms. Some were painted. A few were even put in buildings as works of art. Others were covered with pieces of glass or beads. Some were even covered with gold and jewels.

Dorothy used to travel around the country in her van, called the Eggmobile. She would go from one fair to another showing people her eggs. Just as you might guess, she was welcomed wherever she went.

Unit 3
Eggs, Eggs Everywhere

1. What happened first?
   (A) Dorothy Crall wanted to start an egg museum.
   (B) Dorothy Crall began collecting colored eggs.
   (C) Dorothy Crall began to travel around in her van.

---

2. What did Dorothy Crall start doing at the same time she began her collection?
   (A) Looking for a van
   (B) Coloring eggs herself
   (C) Working on an egg farm

---

3. When did Dorothy Crall begin asking artists to make special eggs?
   (A) Before she began to decorate eggs herself
   (B) After she stopped working
   (C) After she began coloring eggs

---

4. What happened last?
   (A) Dorothy started traveling around the country.
   (B) Dorothy started an egg museum.
   (C) Dorothy started decorating eggs.

Unit 4
Gentle Giants

Jan Samuels spends a great deal of her life underwater. Many days each week, Jan dives into the warm, quiet water of the Crystal River in Florida. There she watches these strange animals. They look like giant gray balloons. "Manatees," she explains, "are very strange. They look like cows, but they live in the sea. They're large, but they are very gentle."

One day Jan slipped over the side of her small boat. She swam across a small bay. She stopped a few feet from two manatees, a mother and her baby, called a calf. Then Jan dived underwater. She swam right up to the large manatee. Next she tickled the animal's stomach. Slowly the manatee rolled onto its back and seemed to smile.

After a few moments, the manatees came up for air. Jan swam with the manatees some more. Suddenly Jan heard a loud noise. It was a motorboat. Signs all around the bay told people that manatees lived here. Boats were supposed to slow down. Someone was not paying attention to the signs!

Quickly Jan pushed the manatees toward shore. It was just in time. A boat came speeding past. "That was lucky," Jan said to herself. "Another few inches, and we would have lost you both."

That night, Jan and her father talked about what had happened. "It's people like that who are making life impossible for manatees," said Jan's father.

Jan and her friends started a special club. The members work to keep manatees safe. They make sure that no one speeds boats near the manatees and that the manatees get enough plants to eat each day. Most of all, the members play with the gentle giants. They want the manatees to stay in their Florida home forever.

Unit 4
Gentle Giants

1. What happened first?
(A) A motorboat raced through the bay.
(B) Jan slipped over the side of her boat.
(C) Jan pushed the manatees toward shore.

2. Before Jan tickled the manatee, what happened?
(A) She made sure they had enough to eat.
(B) She played with them.
(C) She dived underwater.

3. When did Jan decide to help keep manatees safe?
(A) After the motorboat raced by
(B) When she first came to Florida
(C) Before she slipped into the water

4. What happened last?
(A) Jan helped start a special club.
(B) Jan started helping her father.
(C) Jan played with the mother manatee.

Unit 5
Sarah's Project

"What a great idea!" Sarah said to herself. "It'll be the greatest science fair project ever." That afternoon, Sarah got to work. First, she went to the library and came home with a stack of books. Three days later, her older brother drove her to the store. After a while, she returned with some packages.

Sarah worked on her project every afternoon and night. No one knew what it was going to be. Even Jenna, her friend, got the same answer as everyone else: "It's a secret project."

Sarah's family got used to most of what went on. The red and green lights that flashed underneath Sarah's closed door were the only things that bothered anyone. What could she be up to?

"I've hit a problem!" Sarah called as she rushed out the door. "I'm going to the library again."

Three hours later, she was back. Under her arm was a large stack of magazines. "Starting over?" laughed her brother.

"Not at all," Sarah said with a grin. "Just a small problem. It'll all be worked out by the science fair tomorrow."

The next night, Sarah's mother and father drove her to the science fair at school. Sarah carried only a shoe box. "You mean that's what all this fuss has been about?" asked her father.

"Just you wait," Sarah said calmly. "You'll see."

Twenty minutes later, Sarah was showing her project. Dozens of people were standing around, looking closely. The sound of Sarah's voice could be heard. "This is Gizmo, my robot. It walks. It blinks green for **yes.** It blinks red for **no.** Just about the only thing it won't do is my homework."

"I bet she wins first prize," said Sarah's father.

Unit 5
Sarah's Project

1. What happened first?
   (A) Sarah went to the store.
   (B) Sarah went to the library.
   (C) Sarah took a shoe box to the science fair.

2. What happened before Sarah said, "I've hit a problem"?
   (A) She worked every afternoon and night.
   (B) She went back to the library.
   (C) Her mother and father drove her to school.

3. When did Sarah bring home a stack of magazines?
   (A) At the very beginning of the project
   (B) When she found a problem
   (C) After the science fair began

4. What happened last?
   (A) Sarah's father said she would win first prize.
   (B) Sarah showed her project to people.
   (C) Red and green lights flashed under Sarah's door.

Unit 6
Wyland's Whales

One day, people in Honolulu, Hawaii, were greeted by a very unusual sight. A man was making a painting on the side of an apartment building. It was probably the biggest painting any of the people had ever seen.

The painting was the work of an artist named Wyland, from Detroit, Michigan. His art is so large because he paints whales. Making a life-size picture of a whale takes up a lot of space.

Wyland has always loved large animals. Even as a child he was always busy drawing dinosaurs, whales, and other giant creatures. After he finished school, Wyland moved to California. That was where he saw his first real whales. That made him decide to spend part of his time painting these giant animals.

Wyland worked as an artist even before he finished school. At the age of 15, he painted a snowy mountain on the side of an ice-cream store. Then he painted pictures on cars, vans, and trucks. This early work taught him how to make his giant whale pictures.

Before Wyland makes a picture, he drives around the city. He looks for a big empty wall. Then Wyland asks the owner if he can put a picture on the wall—for free. Once Wyland gets an idea for the picture he wants, he starts to work. He covers the whole wall with blue, for the sea and sky. Then he slowly adds to the pictures. The paintings look so real that people often stop in their tracks when they see them.

Why does Wyland make these pictures? He hopes that if people see even a picture of a whale, they will help save the whales from disappearing from Earth.

Unit 6
Wyland's Whales

1. What happened first?
   (A) Wyland moved to California.
   (B) Wyland drew pictures of dinosaurs.
   (C) Wyland painted the side of an ice-cream store.

2. When did Wyland paint a snowy mountain on an ice-cream store?
   (A) When he was 25
   (B) Before he finished school
   (C) After he painted pictures on cars and trucks

3. What does Wyland do before he makes a painting?
   (A) He makes people stop in their tracks.
   (B) He looks for a large empty wall.
   (C) He looks for a whale.

4. What happened last?
   (A) Wyland moved to California.
   (B) Wyland finished school.
   (C) Wyland decided to paint pictures to save the whales.

The First L A P
Language Activity Pages

In Unit 4 you read about someone who spends a great deal of her time in the water. Think about what you know about the sea and the things that live in it. Then read the following.

Teresa slipped on her mask and flippers. Her snorkel still hung from the strap on her mask. Then, with a wave to her mother and father, she slipped into the water. After a moment or two of swimming, she was clear of the boat. Soon, her father was beside her. "Okay," he called, "let's go down."

Putting the soft plastic of the snorkel between her teeth, Teresa moved underwater. For a moment or two, she swam along. Air came to her through the long tube of the snorkel. While she was moving she kept her eyes glued to the bottom of the sea. She hoped she would soon see what she was looking for.

A. Exercising Your Skill

Think about the order in which things happen in this part of the story. What happens first? What happens next? Which words help you know the order in which the events happen?

Now read the list of events below. On your paper, write the events in the order in which they happen in the story.

- Teresa waved to her mother and father.
- Teresa searched the bottom of the sea.
- Teresa put the soft plastic snorkel into her mouth.
- Teresa slipped on her mask and flippers.
- Teresa left the boat.
- Teresa and her father dived below the surface.

B. Expanding Your Skill

What do you think might happen next in this story? List three events that you think might happen. Number them to show the order in which they would take place.

C. Exploring Language

Imagine that you are describing Teresa's adventure. On your paper, write words to complete this part of the story. You may use more than one word in each blank. Pay attention to words in the story that tell you when the events happen.

In a few moments Teresa noticed ______. She came to the surface and waited for her father to appear. Then she told him ______. "Well," he said, "let's go down and check it out."

Seconds later, they were ______. Their hands pushed aside sand and plants. Soon ______. They calmly made their way back to the surface. Filling up with air, they once again ______.

Again and again they ______. At last they could see ______. It really was ______.

When they were back on the surface, Teresa's father called to the boat. "Hey; ______." In a matter of seconds, the boat was next to them. Quickly Teresa's mother tied a balloon to a rope. At the end of the rope was a heavy piece of metal. As soon as she was finished, she ______. It slowly sank to the bottom. "Now," said Teresa's father, "we'll be able to find this spot whenever we want."

D. Expressing Yourself

Choose one of these activities.

1. Think about what Teresa and her father might have found. On your paper, finish the story. As you write it, make sure that your reader will be able to tell exactly when each event takes place.
2. Create a play using the story of Teresa's diving adventure. Include directions that tell the actors what to do—swim, dive, wave, and so on. Make up your own ending for the play.

Unit 7
Jamal Goes Fishing

Jamal Wilson's grandfather laughed when he said, "We'll have to be out of here before five tomorrow. So get yourself to bed."

True to his word, Jamal's grandfather had them out the door a few minutes before five o'clock. After a short drive they parked beside the beach. As they neared the water, Jamal cried out, "Look! There must be 50 people here."

Jamal's grandfather patted the boy on the shoulder. "Don't worry. There's plenty of room, and there will be so many fish you won't even notice anyone else. Come on, let's get going."

The two set up near the water. First, Jamal's grandfather showed the boy how to work the lines on the fishing rods. Next, he showed him how to practice with the long rods.

Suddenly a shout was heard. "Here they come!"

In a flash everyone was down by the water. Jamal could see small waves in the water. "Those are the fish," his grandfather explained. "The little waves are their heads coming to the top. Behind the little fish will come the bluefish. They're chasing the little ones. Just toss your line out there and wait for a bite."

For the next half hour, Jamal did just that. Fish kept coming past, even as the two walked farther out into the water. It seemed as if they would never stop catching fish.

Finally, the fish stopped coming. Jamal had caught six big bluefish. His grandfather had caught several dozen. Slowly they started back to the car. "That was great," Jamal said. "I've never seen anything like it."

"It'll be even better next time," his grandfather winked. "Now let's get these fish cleaned."

Unit 7
Jamal Goes Fishing

1. What happened first?
(A) Jamal learned how to work the lines.
(B) Jamal and his grandfather drove to the beach.
(C) The fish started to come past.

2. What happened after a shout was heard?
(A) Jamal saw the fish.
(B) Jamal practiced with the rods.
(C) They parked beside the beach.

3. When did they walk farther out into the water?
(A) While the fish were coming past
(B) Before the fish came past
(C) After the fish came past

4. What happened last?
(A) They started back to the car.
(B) Jamal's grandfather said they should get the fish cleaned.
(C) Jamal caught six big bluefish.

Unit 8
It's a Shark!

One day not too long ago, a United States Navy boat was at sea near the Hawaiian islands. To keep the boat in place, the sailors used a "sea anchor." A sea anchor is a large piece of cloth shaped like a parachute. A sea anchor keeps a boat in one place when the usual kind of anchor will not reach all the way to the bottom of the sea.

After a while the sailors started to pull in the sea anchor. It was then that they got one of the biggest surprises ever. Caught in the anchor was the largest shark anyone had ever seen. The shark had died trying to swallow the giant piece of cloth.

The sailors pulled the huge shark all the way back to the Navy laboratory on Oahu, a Hawaiian island. There, Navy scientists studied the shark carefully. They knew that the sailors had found something very unusual and very important. However, the scientists were not sure exactly what it was.

The huge shark was called "Megamouth," a name the scientists gave it because of its very large mouth. Inside that mouth were more than 400 small teeth. The shark's mouth was so big that it probably could have swallowed the boat's sea anchor, although certainly not in a single bite!

When the Navy scientist looked into Megamouth's stomach, they found that is was full of tiny shrimp and other tiny sea creatures. The scientists believe that the shark somehow makes a light inside its mouth. This light brings the shrimp into the mouth. Then the shark swallows them, along with the water they swim in. The shark's teeth then strain the shrimp from the water.

Scientists from all over the world have come to study this unusual shark. They hope to learn more about it, and they also hope to come upon other Megamouths. They are sure that there are others somewhere in the sea.

Unit 8
It's a Shark!

1. What happened first?

(A) Scientists studied the shark.

(B) The sailors pulled in a shark.

(C) The sailors used a sea anchor to hold the boat in place.

2. What happened as the sailors pulled in the sea anchor?

(A) They got a big surprise.

(B) They took the shark to Oahu.

(C) They found shrimp in the shark's stomach.

3. When did the shark get the name "Megamouth"?

(A) Before the sailors pulled in the sea anchor

(B) After sailors brought the shark to the laboratory

(C) When scientists looked into the shark's stomach

4. What happened last?

(A) Navy scientists named the shark.

(B) Navy scientists studied what was in the shark's stomach.

(C) Scientists from around the world came to study the shark.

Unit 9
Summer Camp

Some young people dream of spending their summers resting and doing nothing. Ten-year-old Olivia Rodriguez spent her summer in the Rocky Mountains.

Olivia's adventure began when her parents drove her to a camp in Colorado. There she met the other campers and her counselors, the camp leaders. It was not hard to make friends. Everyone was interested in hiking and learning about nature. Everyone wanted to see the wild animals in the mountains.

Olivia was busy the first day. She and some friends went with a counselor to study the nearby tundra. The tundra is land high in the mountains with no trees. Colorado is a wonderful place to look at plants and animals. Olivia found a pika, a tiny furry animal that is even smaller than a mouse. Pikas became some of her favorite animal friends.

A few days later, Olivia was up to her knees in mud. She and some friends had decided to find out about ponds and streams. They waded through mud and water. Beavers took a quick look at what was going on. They hurried back into their homes to hide from the strange, laughing people.

For Olivia the best part of the whole time was their one night away from the camp, when the young people split into small groups. Each group set out in a different van to find its own camping spot. They drove and hiked for miles. At last Olivia and her friends found a wonderful spot. They spent the afternoon looking for deer. Then they cooked a delicious meal on open fires. Finally they fell into their sleeping bags, ready for bed.

Now, months later, Olivia keeps a picture of her camp friends in her room at home. "It helps me plan for next summer," she says. "There's a trail that goes way up into the mountains that I would love to try to hike."

Unit 9
Summer Camp

1. What happened first?
   (A) Olivia spent a night away from the camp.
   (B) Olivia looked for plants and animals on the tundra.
   (C) The campers learned about ponds and streams.

2. When did the beavers see Olivia?
   (A) Before she saw the pika
   (B) After her group found a camping spot
   (C) While she waded through mud and water

3. What did the young people do before they split into groups?
   (A) They drove in vans for miles and miles.
   (B) They looked for deer.
   (C) They waded through mud.

4. What happened last?
   (A) Olivia found a wonderful spot.
   (B) Olivia and her friends cooked on an open fire.
   (C) Olivia fell asleep in her sleeping bag.

Unit 10
Fish Out of Water

Each spring and early summer, people from all over come to the beaches of California. They come to see one of the most unusual sights in the world. They want to see what happens when "the grunions are running." As people stand in the cool night air, thousands of jumping, wiggling fish make their way from the water to the beach. These fish are the "grunions." They come to the shore on the two or three nights around each full or new moon. That is when the tide is at its highest point.

Grunions are small silvery fish about six inches long. In most ways they are just like other fish. However, when it is time to lay their eggs, grunions make this strange journey out of the water. In the middle of the night, as soon as the water is at its highest point, the grunions ride in on the waves and land on the beach. Then they wiggle their way up the beach. All the while, they make faint squeaks and grunts, similar to sounds that pigs make. These noises gave the fish their name. Early Spanish settlers called the fish *gruñon,* which means "grunter."

The grunions wiggle their way as far from the ocean as they can. Then the female fish start to move their tails back and forth. This helps them dig themselves down into the soft, wet sand. Soon, only the tiny heads of the fish can be seen. Then, in just a few seconds, each fish lays almost 3,000 eggs.

Quickly, the male grunions hurry to where the eggs have just been placed to fertilize them. Then, hurrying as fast as they can, the grunions wiggle themselves back to the ocean.

It all takes no more than 30 seconds. In another ten days, when the water is at its highest point once again, waves wash the eggs out to sea. Finally the eggs hatch, and the baby grunions swim away.

Unit 10
Fish Out of Water

1. What happens first?

(A) The female grunions lay their eggs.

(B) The grunions wiggle their way up the beach.

(C) The water reaches its highest point.

---

2. Before the grunions come to the shore, what happens?

(A) The eggs are buried in the sand.

(B) There is either a full or new moon.

(C) Ten days go by.

---

3. When do the females dig themselves into the sand?

(A) After the males fertilize the eggs

(B) After they wiggle up the beach

(C) Before the water reaches its highest point

---

4. What happens last?

(A) The eggs hatch.

(B) High waters come to the shore again.

(C) The eggs wash out to sea.

Unit 11
The Cuckoo Bird

In North America a bird called the cuckoo raises its babies the same way other birds do. The cuckoos make a nest and put their eggs in the nest. Then, when the eggs hatch, the parents take care of the baby cuckoos until they are grown. Cuckoos in Europe, though, are very different. They let other birds take care of their babies.

When a European cuckoo is ready to lay her eggs, she does not build a nest. Instead she looks for another bird's nest. She needs to find one nest for each of her eggs.

After she has found a nest, the cuckoo waits until the other mother bird leaves her nest for a while. Quickly the mother cuckoo sneaks into the nest and removes one of the other bird's eggs. As fast as she can, the cuckoo lays one of her own eggs in its place. Then before the other bird gets back, the cuckoo flies off to find the next nest.

When the other bird returns, she never notices the cuckoo's egg in her nest. In fact, she sits on it along with her own eggs. Later, when the egg hatches, she cares for the young cuckoo as if it were her own.

The young cuckoo often hatches before the other eggs. It starts to push the other eggs and young birds out of the nest. After a while the mother bird has fewer babies to care for. This means more food for the young cuckoo.

After about three weeks the young cuckoo is ready to fly from the nest. Next spring, it will have babies of its own—and have some other bird take care of them!

Unit 11
The Cuckoo Bird

1. What happens first?
   (A) The cuckoo pushes other eggs from the nest.
   (B) The other bird takes care of the baby cuckoo.
   (C) The mother cuckoo sneaks into a nest.

2. What does the mother cuckoo do before she lays her own egg?
   (A) She feeds the other birds.
   (B) She builds herself a nest.
   (C) She removes one of the other bird's eggs.

3. What happens when the egg hatches?
   (A) The other bird leaves the young cuckoo.
   (B) The other bird cares for the young cuckoo.
   (C) The other bird gives the young cuckoo to its mother.

4. What happens last?
   (A) The other bird returns to its nest and eggs.
   (B) The cuckoo places its egg in the nest.
   (C) The young cuckoo is ready to fly from its nest.

Unit 12
Emma Anders Reporting

Emma Anders rushed from the field. She was thinking about her story as she ran. It would be a good story. Emma was sure. Maybe this story would win a prize too.

Emma is a reporter for the Davis High School newspaper. She writes about all the sports teams. Emma is busy every season. In the fall Emma writes about football games and track meets. In the winter, basketball games and swim meets keep Emma busy. She goes to both the girls' and boys' games and to every swim meet. In the spring Emma needs a helper. She can't get to every baseball game, track meet, and tennis match by herself.

Today the Davis High baseball team became state champions. Emma's story must be ready in two days. The school newspaper comes out on Thursday, and Emma's story must be ready one day earlier. Emma hopes her story will be as good as one she wrote last November. The Davis High football team became state champions last fall. Emma's story won a prize then. The story appeared in the town newspaper too.

On the ride home from the game, Emma read her notes. Then, when she got home, she wrote her story on the computer. When it was finished, she read it one more time. She wanted to ask her mother or father to read it to check her work. Emma printed the story and took it downstairs.

Emma's dad read the story slowly. He marked three places where Emma needed to change some things. Dad thought Emma might use different words in those places.

"It's a very good story, Emma. It lets everyone know how excited the players and fans were. You make me feel as though I was there. You also tell all the facts," Dad said proudly. "Every story you write is better than the one before. Just fix those few sentences I marked, and maybe this story will be in the town paper too."

Unit 12
Emma Anders Reporting

1. What happened first?
   (A) Davis High became baseball champions.
   (B) Davis High became football champions.
   (C) Emma's story was in the town paper.

2. Before Emma writes a story, what does she do?
   (A) She shows it to her parents.
   (B) She makes notes.
   (C) She prints the story.

3. After a game what does Emma do first?
   (A) She writes her story.
   (B) She reads her story one more time.
   (C) She reads her notes.

4. What happened last?
   (A) The baseball team became state champions.
   (B) Emma's dad helped her with her story.
   (C) Emma rushed from the field.

The Second L A P
Language Activity Pages

In Unit 7 you read about Jamal Wilson and his grandfather going fishing. Now read about how some other grandparents wanted to keep water clean for their grandchildren.

For 30 years, Ellen and Gus Ransom had worked in their family's grocery store. Finally the two decided that they did not want to work anymore. Their two sons took over the store. Ellen and Gus thought they would have time to rest.

But things started happening soon after the two stopped working. One day they were reading a news story about a trash plant the town wanted to build right down by the beach.

After reading the news story, the two decided to do something about it. "We can't have all that garbage right where our grandchildren go swimming," Ellen said. And from that moment on, they worked to stop the trash plant from being built there.

A. Exercising Your Skill

Think about the order in which things happen in this part of the story. Now read the mixed-up list of events below. On your paper, write the events in the order in which they happen in the story.

- The Ransoms read a news story about a new trash plant.
- The Ransoms turned their store over to their children.
- The Ransoms decided to stop the new trash plant from being built.
- The Ransoms ran a family grocery store.
- The Ransoms worried about trash and garbage at the town beach.

B. Expanding Your Skill

What do you think might happen next in this story? Write three events that you think might happen. Number them to show the order in which they would take place.

C. Exploring Language

Imagine that you live in Seaview, where the Ransoms live. What do you think they did to stop the trash plant? Do you think they were able to stop it?

On your paper, write the words that complete this part of the story. You may use more than one word in each blank. Pay attention to words in the story that tell you when the events happen.

> Like many other people in Seaview, the Ransoms were upset about the new trash plant. Over the past years the beach had been ______.
>
> "All that will be ruined!" Ellen told her neighbors. "Think of all that garbage right where we will be swimming."
>
> Soon the neighbors ______. After a week a meeting ______. More than 50 people ______. After the meeting, ______. Soon people wrote letters to ______. At the same time they ______. After a few weeks a woman from the mayor's office came to a meeting at the Ransoms' house. At first she______. But in the end ______. The next day the Ransoms told the town newspaper that ______.

D. Expressing Yourself

Choose one of these activities.

1. Imagine that people will tell how they feel about the trash plant at the meeting. Write a list of four or five reasons in favor of having the plant. Then write four or five reasons against having the plant.
2. Write a newspaper story about how the Ransoms stopped the trash plant. Your story should tell what happened, where it happened, when it happened, why it happened, and how it happened.

Unit 13
Batter Up!

Kelley Daniels stared at the batter. Behind her she could hear her team cheering her on. Then with a smooth movement, she sent the ball toward the plate. She smiled and threw her hand in the air as the man in blue called, "Strike two!"

It had not been easy for Kelley to become the star pitcher of her baseball team. In fact, there had been concern when she first tried to join the team. People were afraid of having a girl on the team. "What if she gets hurt?" everyone had asked.

Finally Kelley's parents told everyone that there was no need to worry. Even more important, Kelley soon showed the team that she could play just as well as anyone else. She could pitch. She could hit. "I'm not the greatest base runner," she told her coach with a laugh. "But if I hit the ball hard enough, it doesn't really matter, does it?"

Now, Kelley's team, the Birds, was fighting to win first place over all the other teams. Just before the game with the Tigers, Coach Matthews had come to her. "You're pitching today, Kelley. How do you feel about that?"

Kelley swallowed hard. For a moment she wanted to say that she wasn't good enough. However, she knew she was the best pitcher on the team. "Great," she said. "I'll give it my best."

After half the game was over, the score was tied. Then Kelley hit a home run. Could the Birds hold on to their lead? Next two Tigers got on base, but no one scored. Kelley's teammate Mateo made a great catch at second base. Then Kelley struck out the last batter.

It was the end of the game. Kelley had to get just one more batter out. Once more she stared at the batter. She threw a pitch. The batter swung. It was a slow ground ball. Mateo picked up the ball and tossed it to first base. It was over! Kelley had pitched her team to first place.

Unit 13
Batter Up!

1. What happened first?
   (A) People worried that Kelley might get hurt.
   (B) Kelley's parents talked with people.
   (C) Kelley tried to join the team.

2. When was the score tied?
   (A) After half the game was over
   (B) After two Tigers got on base
   (C) After Kelley hit a home run

3. What happened after Mateo made a great catch?
   (A) The score was tied.
   (B) Kelley struck out the last Tiger batter.
   (C) Kelley hit a home run.

4. What happened last?
   (A) Mateo tossed the ball to first.
   (B) The batter hit a slow ground ball.
   (C) Kelley hit a home run.

Unit 14
Emergency, Please

Sue Doleshal walked into the room where the Wild Animal Park's gorillas sleep. In the room Sue found Dolly, one of the gorillas, acting strangely. Sue rushed to the phone. As quickly as she could, she called the hospital.

Within moments Dr. Don Janssen arrived. He was the zoo's doctor. Quickly Janssen used a special device to shoot medicine into Dolly. Soon the giant gorilla was sound asleep.

Dr. Janssen and the other keepers worked as fast as they could. Dolly was checked from head to foot. Finally, the doctors knew what was wrong.

Dolly had a large swelling inside her stomach. The swelling had to be taken out. Three days later, Dr. Janssen and the keepers once again used sleeping medicine on Dolly. Then they carried her outside to a special van. Soon several doctors began to work on Dolly.

The doctors took 15 minutes to remove the swelling. Within days Dolly began to feel better. She started to eat again. She moved around more. She even started to play a little. After a few more days of rest, Dolly was ready to take care of her baby, Schroeder, once more.

The keepers made a special gate so Schroeder could come and visit his mother. As soon as she saw the young gorilla, Dolly perked right up. And she grew stronger every day.

Soon Dolly and Schroeder were together again, climbing and playing in front of hundreds of happy visitors. Sue Doleshal watched them and smiled.

Unit 14
Emergency, Please

1. What happened first?
   (A) Dolly got a "shot" of sleeping medicine.
   (B) Sue Doleshal called the hospital.
   (C) Dr. Janssen came to the gorilla area.

2. What happened just after Dr. Janssen arrived?
   (A) Keepers made a special gate.
   (B) Dr. Janssen shot medicine into Dolly.
   (C) Dolly began to act strangely.

3. When did the doctors remove the swelling?
   (A) Three days after Dr. Janssen checked over Dolly
   (B) A week after Sue Doleshal called the hospital
   (C) A few days before the gorilla fell asleep

4. What happened last?
   (A) Keepers carried Dolly to a van.
   (B) Dolly got sick.
   (C) Dolly climbed and played again.

Unit 15
Yolanda Bergman, "Food Cop"

Yolanda Bergman helps people with their food. She can help them eat less. She can make sure they keep away from foods that are not good for them. She can even cook special meals for people and deliver the meals to them. Yolanda Bergman says she is a one-person "police department" for food.

Bergman did not start out in life as a "food cop." When she was young, she loved to dance. Later she became a dancer for a while. Then she moved to California. There she took a job as an exercise teacher. After a few years she opened her own exercise business. She and three other teachers taught classes and helped people keep in shape.

During this time Bergman learned how to cook meals that are delicious and healthful, or good for you. What is more, these meals did not make people gain weight. Soon her exercise business and her cooking came together. Some of her exercise students asked for help with what they ate. Bergman was soon making breakfasts, dinners, and even snacks. In about two years, she had more than 35 people working with her.

How does Bergman do it? For some people she just has to bring them the right food. One, two, or even three times each day she takes people their meals. Each meal is specially made for the person's needs.

How do the people she works for feel about this? Well, more and more people are coming to her each month. In fact she now takes care of some famous people in movies, television, and music. But Bergman does not want to stop there. She wants to make sure people eat good food even when she is not around.

Unit 15
Yolanda Bergman, "Food Cop"

1. What happened first?
   (A) Bergman opened her own exercise business.
   (B) Bergman moved to California.
   (C) Bergman opened restaurants all around the country.

2. What did Bergman do before she became an exercise teacher?
   (A) She was a dancer.
   (B) She cooked delicious, healthful food.
   (C) She owned restaurants.

3. How long did it take until 35 people worked with her?
   (A) About three days
   (B) About three years
   (C) About two years

4. What happened last?
   (A) Bergman started cooking special meals.
   (B) Famous people came to Bergman for help.
   (C) Bergman took a job as an exercise teacher.

Unit 16
Surf's Up!

Surfing is the name for riding ocean waves on special boards. Did you know that surfing has been around for more than 200 years? At first the sport was rougher and harder than it is today.

For one thing the early surfboards were heavy. They weighed as much as 150 pounds. A surfer needed great strength just to get the board from the beach to the water! Also the early surfers didn't ride standing up. They rode just lying on their stomachs. That was the only way to control the large boards.

Those surfers lived in the islands of Polynesia, in the South Pacific. In 1778 the surfers took the sport to Hawaii. There surfing quickly became popular. The beaches and waves of Hawaii are perfect for surfing.

In 1907 George Freeth was the first person to ride a wave in the United States. He surfed in Redondo Beach in California.

For years the sport of surfing spread slowly. In the 1950s surfing was known as a young people's sport because mostly young people seemed to enjoy it. In 1961 rules for surfers were written. The surfers themselves, along with some surfboard companies, made up the rules.

Today surfers are looked upon as athletes. Southern California is still the surfing center of the United States. Thousands of people surf there. Thousands more are fans of famous surfers. Surfing is here to stay.

Surfers must still be strong. To surf, a person should be able to swim well, both on top of and under the water. A surfer must also be able to float for a long time. A good surfer must keep his or her eyes open at all times, even underwater.

Unit 16
Surf's Up!

1. What happened first?

(A) Surfing spread slowly.

(B) Surfing was taken to Hawaii.

(C) George Freeth went surfing.

---

2. What took place before the 1950s?

(A) Rules for surfers were written.

(B) Surfers were looked upon as athletes.

(C) Surfboards weighed 150 pounds.

---

3. When was surfing known as a young people's sport?

(A) In the 1950s

(B) In 1907

(C) In 1778

---

4. What happened last?

(A) People in Polynesia surfed on heavy boards.

(B) Surfers didn't ride standing up.

(C) Surfers wrote their own rules.

Unit 17
Bears, Bears, Bears

Bears sometimes leave their forest homes and come into the city. They do that because they are looking for food.

When a bear leaves the woods and comes into a city, forest workers come with a cage and put the bear into it. Next they put the cage on a truck. Then they drive the truck into the woods. They set the bear free when they finally reach very deep woods.

Bears can cause trouble in parks too. They take picnic baskets full of food. A hungry bear with a basket of food is in a bit of a hurry, so it doesn't bother opening the lid. It first throws the basket on the ground to break it open. Then, when the basket is ruined, it is the bear's lunchtime.

Here is a story from the Great Smoky Mountain National Park. A black bear in that park discovered an outdoor candy machine. The chocolate and nuts must have smelled like honey to the bear. The bear probably thought of the machine as a big picnic basket. He tore it apart like a basket, anyway. Then he ate the candy and left.

The person who owned the candy machine put a new machine in its place. To keep the bear out, the owner wrapped a heavy chain around the middle of the machine.

The next morning the owner came to check on the machine. The chain was still wrapped around the middle of it. The candy, however, was gone. Do you know what the bear had done? First, he had grabbed the top of the door. Then, he bent it right down over the chain. In other words, the bear folded a metal door in half!

We should remember that bears in the woods eat such things as berries, honey, and fish. When they are around people, though, bears start to want foods such as sandwiches and apple pies. That's when bear trouble begins.

Unit 17
Bears, Bears, Bears

1. What happened first?
   (A) The bear folded a metal door in half.
   (B) The bear discovered a candy machine.
   (C) The owner wrapped a chain around the machine.

2. What did the bear do after smelling the chocolate and nuts?
   (A) Went looking for berries
   (B) Dropped the basket
   (C) Tore the machine apart

3. What did the owner do after the bear ate the candy?
   (A) Chased the bear
   (B) Fixed the machine
   (C) Put in a new machine

4. What happened last?
   (A) The bear folded the metal door in half.
   (B) The bear grabbed the top of a door.
   (C) The bear took off the chain.

Unit 18
Sidney Poitier

Sidney Poitier is an actor and movie director. He was born in Florida and grew up in the Bahamas, a group of islands south of Florida. He served in an army medical unit during World War II. Then he moved to New York to study acting.

Poitier applied to the American Negro Theatre but was turned down. Even though he is African American, his years in the Bahamas had given him an "islands accent." He listened to American radio and practiced speaking with the voices he heard there. Then he applied again and was accepted.

His first starring role on Broadway was in 1959. He played in *Raisin in the Sun* by Lorraine Hansberry. It was the first popular play to describe African American life to a wide theater audience.

Poitier went on to star in many movies. Two of his well-known films are *Blackboard Jungle* and *In the Heat of the Night.* In 1963 he won an Oscar for best actor for his role in the film *Lilies of the Field.* Poitier eventually directed many films.

Poitier has won many awards throughout his career. In 1995 he won a Kennedy Center Award. The award recognized his talents for acting and directing. It also brought attention to Poitier's great work for equal rights.

Unit 18
Sidney Poitier

1. What happened first?
(A) Sidney Poitier joined the army.
(B) Sidney Poitier changed his accent.
(C) Sidney Poitier lived in the Bahamas.

---

2. When did Sidney Poitier first star on Broadway?
(A) Before he studied with the American Negro Theatre
(B) After he made several movies
(C) After his study of American radio accents

---

3. When did Sidney Poitier begin directing movies?
(A) After he won the Oscar
(B) Before he starred on Broadway
(C) After he won the Kennedy Center Award

---

4. What happened last?
(A) Sidney Poitier won a Kennedy Center Award.
(B) Sidney Poitier starred in *In the Heat of the Night.*
(C) Sidney Poitier won an Oscar.

Unit 19
Left Behind

Almost 300 years ago, a tall man raced along the island beach. "Wait for me!" he cried. "I've changed my mind!"

The man was Alexander Selkirk. He was calling to a ship called the *Cinque Ports,* which means the "Five Ports." Earlier Selkirk had decided to stay on the island. He changed his mind at the last second, when the ship set sail. But it was too late. Now Selkirk was alone on an island in the Pacific Ocean.

The next day Selkirk walked around the island. There were caves to use for shelter, and streams for washing. There were fruit trees, wild goats, and fish. Selkirk could use all of these for food. However, there were no people. Selkirk was truly alone.

That island in the Pacific was Selkirk's home for more than four years. He kept hoping for someone to come and take him from the island.

Finally a British ship sailed to the island, and Selkirk was saved. He went home to Scotland and told his story. Newspapers told about his adventure.

One man who read about Selkirk was the writer Daniel Defoe. He then turned Selkirk's story into a book called *The Strange and Surprising Adventures of Robinson Crusoe.* In the book, Robinson Crusoe lived the way Selkirk did, with one big difference. Crusoe had a friend, a man called Friday.

Today you can find the book about Robinson Crusoe in any library. Few books, however, tell the story of the "real" Robinson Crusoe—the man named Alexander Selkirk.

Unit 19
Left Behind

1. What happened first?

(A) Selkirk was alone on the island.

(B) The *Cinque Ports* left the island.

(C) Selkirk decided to stay on the island.

2. When did Selkirk walk around the island?

(A) Before he called to the *Cinque Ports*

(B) After the *Cinque Ports* left the island

(C) Before he changed his mind

3. When did Selkirk leave the island?

(A) When the story of his adventure became a book

(B) After he had been there for four years

(C) On the day after the *Cinque Ports* set sail

4. What happened last?

(A) Daniel Defoe wrote *Robinson Crusoe.*

(B) The British ship saved Selkirk.

(C) Newspapers told Selkirk's story.

A. Exercising Your Skill

In Unit 17 you learned that bears like honey. If you are like many other people, you like honey too. Have you ever tried following a recipe that uses honey? If you have, you know that recipes list all the steps you must follow when you cook something. The steps are given in a certain order. If you do not follow the order, the recipe may not come out right. Often the steps in a recipe are numbered 1, 2, 3, and so on.

Read the following recipe carefully. Are the steps in the correct order?

Toasted Honey-Sesame Sticks

- Sprinkle one tablespoon of sesame seeds on the honey-buttered bread sticks.
- Slice each piece of bread into four sticks.
- Toast the honey-sesame bread sticks in an oven at 400°F until they are done (about 8 minutes).
- After cutting the bread, mix together one tablespoon of melted butter and two tablespoons of honey.
- Cut the crusts off two slices of bread.
- Spread each bread stick with the honey-butter mix.

You could probably tell that the steps are not in order. Number your paper from *1* to *6*. Next to each number, write the underlined word for the correct step. For example, after 1 write the underlined word in the step that should happen first.

B. Expanding Your Skill

Compare your recipes with your classmates' recipes. How many classmates listed the steps in the same order that you did? How many did not? Talk about your differences, and see if you can agree on the correct order.

C. Exploring Language

In recipes and other kinds of directions, signal words like *first, second, then, now, after,* and *last* can help make the order of the steps clear.

Read the directions below. Think of four signal words to complete the directions. Write the signal words on your paper in the order they should be used.

_______ pour about four inches of colored water into each of two glasses. _______ put one stalk of celery into each glass. _______ move one of the glasses under a lighted lamp. Keep the other glass far away from any lamp. _______ watch both celery stalks. You will see that the colored water in the glass under the lamp will move up the celery stalk faster than the colored water in the other glass.

D. Expressing Yourself

Choose one of these activities.

1. Choose a favorite recipe or directions for doing something. Write the recipe or directions in an order that does not make sense. Ask a classmate to write the recipe or directions in the correct order.
2. Make up a simple game that two people can play. It can be a guessing game, a board game, a ball game—anything you wish. Think carefully about how to play the game. Then write the directions. Write them very clearly in their correct order, using signal words such as *first, then, after,* and *next.* Give the directions to two classmates, and see how well they can follow them. Do they understand each step? Did you leave out any steps?

Unit 20
Selling the Statue

Not everyone was excited by the Statue of Liberty at first. That is hard to believe now, but it is true.

Fréderic Bartholdi lived in France. He wanted to build the statue, a figure of a woman named Liberty, and give it to America. He visited America in 1871 and shared his idea. Everyone thought the idea was good, but no one did anything. Bartholdi went back to France, still hopeful.

In 1876, the United States was 100 years old. A birthday party took place in the city of Philadelphia. The party was called an Exhibition. That means that people from all over get together and show things they are proud of. Fréderic Bartholdi brought part of his statue to Philadelphia. The part he brought was the huge arm holding a torch (a tool that holds a light of fire). Many people thought the arm and torch made no sense. They didn't understand that the whole statue had not been built yet.

Then Bartholdi took the statue to New York. He needed to get money for the base it would stand on. (He had told the Americans that they would have to pay for the base.)

People in New York weren't sure about the arm and the torch either. "Fine," Bartholdi said. "I'll make the statue a gift to Philadelphia." Then all of a sudden, New York wanted the statue.

The money problem was settled by a newspaper. The *New York World* printed stories about the statue and the base. The stories told people to be good Americans and send money. Good Americans did just that. Many of them were children. Soon the paper collected enough money to pay for the base. In 1886 the statue was completed, base and all.

Unit 20
Selling the Statue

1. What happened first?
   (A) Bartholdi brought part of his statue to Philadelphia.
   (B) The *New York World* printed stories about the base.
   (C) The whole statue was built.

2. Where did Bartholdi take the arm and torch after Philadelphia?
   (A) To France
   (B) To New York
   (C) To the birthday party

3. When did Bartholdi say he'd give the statue to Philadelphia?
   (A) When the money problem was settled
   (B) When New York asked for the statue
   (C) When people in New York weren't sure about the statue

4. What happened last?
   (A) The newspaper collected money for the base.
   (B) The United States had a birthday party.
   (C) The statue was finished.

Unit 21
Learning to Fly

Astronauts, people who fly into space, need special training. First they go to Houston, Texas. That is the home of the Johnson Space Center. There they are tested to see how strong and smart they are.

One of the first tests is for the heart. The person walks or runs. Next the space doctors see how fast her heart is beating.

Then another important test is performed. In this test the person must curl her body up in a ball. Then when she is in that shape, she is put into a round cloth bag. The doctors give her no idea how long she will have to stay in the bag. If a spaceship broke down in space, the astronauts would get into bags like these. Then they would have to wait, curled up in darkness, until help could arrive. You can see that an astronaut must not be afraid of tight spaces or of darkness.

After the tests, only the best people are chosen to start astronaut training in a training center. The astronauts in training learn many other things. They learn how to jump out of a moving airplane. They learn to blow up a rubber lifeboat and get in it while they are in the ocean. The astronauts also have to learn how to get lifted out of the ocean by a helicopter. That may look like fun, but it can be dangerous.

After they finish training, the astronauts continue to work. They stay in good shape by running and doing exercises. They read about their special jobs. That way they can learn new facts about space travel.

Then the big day comes. The astronaut is told to go to work on a flight into space. The crew members get to know each other first. Then they learn which jobs each will do.

Unit 21
Learning to Fly

1. What happens first?
   (A) Doctors do tests on the astronauts.
   (B) The astronauts go to the Space Center.
   (C) The astronauts run and do other exercises.

2. What do the doctors test first?
   (A) The heart
   (B) Fear of tight spaces
   (C) Seeing in the dark

3. What happens next after the tests?
   (A) The astronauts learn about spaceships.
   (B) The best people are chosen for training.
   (C) They curl up in cloth bags.

4. What happens last?
   (A) The astronaut learns how everything on a spaceship works.
   (B) The astronaut learns how to jump out of an airplane.
   (C) The astronaut goes to work on a flight in space.

Unit 22
First in the Sky

The Bessie Coleman Aero Club was formed in Los Angeles in 1929. It was the first all-black flying association. It was named after Bessie Coleman, a pioneering African American flier.

Just a few years before, Bessie Coleman was working as a beautician in Chicago. It was about 1915, during World War I. She watched newsreel films of military fliers and decided she wanted to learn how to fly.

But Coleman had to overcome two obstacles. She was both female and African American. Few people believed African Americans or women should be allowed to fly a plane. No flight school in the United States would give flying lessons to Coleman. So she saved her money, and in 1921 she went to Europe to learn from French fliers.

Bessie Coleman eventually earned her pilot's license in France. She was the first African American woman in the world to do so. Then she returned to America to start a flight school for African American men and women.

In order to earn money for her school, Bessie Coleman flew in air shows. She and other pilots performed exciting stunts in the air. The crowds loved it.

Stunt flying was very dangerous. One day in 1926, Coleman's plane went into a nosedive. She was not wearing her seat belt. She fell from the plane and was killed. For years, African American pilots flew over her grave each Memorial Day. They dropped flowers to honor the woman who had paved the way for them.

Unit 22
First in the Sky

1. What happened first?
   (A) Pilots flew over Coleman's grave.
   (B) Coleman learned how to fly in France.
   (C) Coleman performed in air shows.

---

2. What happened while Coleman was working as a beautician?
   (A) She was also learning how to fly.
   (B) She was also earning money for flight school.
   (C) She was also watching newsreels of military fliers.

---

3. Which of these did Coleman do last?
   (A) She flew in air shows.
   (B) She decided to open a flight school.
   (C) She went to Europe.

---

4. What happened last?
   (A) Coleman fell from her plane.
   (B) Many African Americans became pilots.
   (C) The Bessie Coleman Aero Club was formed.

Unit 23
Hard to Get

A large bird circles overhead. The bird is a hawk. Suddenly the hawk drops from the sky. It has seen an animal it wants to catch. The animal gets away, though. Do you know why? It's because the animal is a prairie dog.

A prairie dog is about the size of a rabbit. Its body is brown and a little like a squirrel's. Prairie dogs live in groups called villages. Their homes are holes in the ground called burrows. The prairie dogs dig the burrows themselves.

One of the best things about prairie dogs is their alarm system. A prairie dog spends a lot of time sitting at the opening of its burrow. While sitting, it watches and listens. Then at the first sign of an enemy, like the hawk, the prairie dog barks.

When one prairie dog barks, other prairie dogs join in. When the hawk dives, it is no surprise to the prairie dogs. They have warned each other. They wait until the last second, as if playing a game. Then they disappear into their burrows. Finally the hawk flies away.

Prairie dogs don't always escape danger, however. Coyotes, which are like wild dogs, hunt prairie dogs. Two coyotes will hunt together and trick the prairie dogs. First, one coyote hides. Next, the other coyote trots through the village of the prairie dogs. After the prairie dogs dive into their holes, the hidden coyote comes out quietly. Then it sneaks up close to a burrow and lies there.

When the prairie dogs cannot hear the coyote moving, they poke their heads out of their burrows. The coyote waits near a burrow. It grabs a prairie dog. This is one time that the alarm system of the prairie dog doesn't work.

Unit 23
Hard to Get

1. What happens first?
   (A) The prairie dog gets away.
   (B) The hawk dives to the ground.
   (C) The hawk circles in the sky.

---

2. Which of these things happens last?
   (A) The prairie dogs watch and listen.
   (B) The prairie dogs disappear into their holes.
   (C) The prairie dogs bark a warning.

---

3. When does the hidden coyote come out quietly?
   (A) Before the other coyote trots through the village
   (B) As the other coyote trots through the village
   (C) After the prairie dogs dive into their holes

---

4. What happens last?
   (A) The coyote grabs a prairie dog.
   (B) The coyote waits by a burrow.
   (C) The prairie dogs decide all is clear.

Unit 24
Georgia O'Keeffe

You may have seen some paintings by Georgia O'Keeffe. Many are pictures of flowers. The flowers are big, bright, and beautiful. O'Keeffe once said, "Filling space in a beautiful way—that is what art is to me."

Georgia O'Keeffe grew up in Wisconsin about 100 years ago. Then, as a young woman, she taught art in the state of Texas. From Texas, O'Keeffe went to New York. She spent her winters in the city. There she painted city scenes, like bridges and tall buildings. In the summers she lived in the country. She stayed at a place called Lake George, New York. She painted pictures of barns and country buildings around Lake George.

In 1929 Georgia O'Keeffe began to spend her summers in New Mexico. The land there looked much like the Texas she remembered. In New Mexico, O'Keeffe painted some of her prettiest flowers. She also painted the bones of animals that had died in the desert. She painted the desert itself, with its open land and red hills. These paintings of New Mexico helped make Georgia O'Keeffe famous.

The year 1971 brought trouble to O'Keeffe's life. She had always been able to see very clearly. In that year, however, her eyes grew weak, and everything she looked at was blurred. This is a terrible thing to happen to an artist.

Even then though, she did not give up painting. She saw pictures in her mind. So she found people who would paint the pictures she described. With those people helping her, O'Keeffe spent her last years doing what she loved best—filling space in a beautiful way. When she died in 1986, Georgia O'Keeffe was 99 years old, and she had been painting for nearly 70 years.

Unit 24
Georgia O'Keeffe

1. What happened first?
   (A) O'Keeffe moved to New York.
   (B) O'Keeffe grew up in Wisconsin.
   (C) O'Keeffe taught art in Texas.

2. When did O'Keeffe paint pictures of barns?
   (A) Before she went to Lake George
   (B) While she was at Lake George
   (C) After she left Lake George

3. When did O'Keeffe begin going to New Mexico?
   (A) Before she went to New York
   (B) After she went to Lake George
   (C) After trouble came to her life

4. What happened last?
   (A) O'Keeffe's eyes grew weak.
   (B) O'Keeffe painted pictures of Texas.
   (C) O'Keeffe became famous.

Unit 25
The Five Nations

Long before there was a United States or Canada, the Iroquois started their own country. Their country, or nation, was called the Five Nations of the Iroquois. Five Native American tribes formed this nation.

The Five Nations was formed by an Iroquois chief named Hiawatha. To get the Iroquois nation started, Hiawatha visited the five tribes and talked to their members. He told them that his ideas came from another Native American. However, no one knew much about him. He may simply have been a storyteller who gave Hiawatha a good plan. Hiawatha, however, made him sound like a person who knew what was best. That made the tribes want to follow Hiawatha's plan.

Before the year 1570, the Five Nations of the Iroquois was formed. The tribes agreed to work together for the good of each other. This meant that they stopped fighting among themselves. They also decided not to go to war with anyone else unless all five tribes voted to do so.

Then, in 1603, the Iroquois tribes were attacked by a group of Canadian Indians. A man named Champlain, who had come from France, helped the Canadians. After the attack by Champlain, the tribes of the Iroquois declared France an enemy. Later when France and England fought for North America, all the Iroquois tribes but one fought on England's side. By doing this the Iroquois helped the English, not the French, settle in America.

Today most of the Iroquois are citizens, or people under the government, of the United States. Next to a lake in New York State is the headquarters of the Iroquois. The nation is smaller than before. Many young Iroquois moved away to go to school and take jobs. All Iroquois people, however, always remain members of the Five Nations of the Iroquois.

Unit 25
The Five Nations

1. What happened first?
   (A) Hiawatha shared his ideas with the members.
   (B) Hiawatha visited the five tribes.
   (C) The tribe members followed Hiawatha's plan.

2. When did Champlain attack the Iroquois?
   (A) After the Five Nations was formed
   (B) Before Hiawatha talked to the storyteller
   (C) As Hiawatha was visiting tribes

3. What did the Iroquois tribes do after Champlain's attack?
   (A) The tribes stopped fighting one another.
   (B) The tribes agreed to work for each other.
   (C) The tribes declared France an enemy.

4. What happened last?
   (A) The Iroquois started their nation.
   (B) The Iroquois fought the French.
   (C) Iroquois headquarters was built in New York State.

The Last L A P
Language Activity Pages

A. Exercising Your Skill

The order in which things happen is called the **sequence.** For example, you learned in Unit 21 that people who want to become astronauts *first* go to Houston, Texas. *Next,* they take some tests. *Then,* they go to a training center for a year.

The three sentences above are written in a sequence that tells what happens first, what happens next, and so on. The words *first, next,* and *then* are clues, or signal words. They tell us the order in which things happen. Some other signal words are *now, before, after, later, last,* and *finally.*

Read the story below. Decide on three good signal words to complete the story. Write the signal words in order on your paper.

How Birds Fly

Birds can fly only when they move their wings. Here's how. _______ the bird lifts its wings upward. When it does this, the bird's feathers spread apart. When the wings are fully raised, the feathers press tightly together. No air can pass between them. _______ the bird moves its wings downward. _______ the bird moves forward.

B. Expanding Your Skill

Exchange your copy of the story above with a classmate's copy. Check to see which signal words your classmate used. Have one or more students write the story on the board. Working as a class, decide which signal words work best.

C. Exploring Language

Read the story events in Part 1 below. Decide on the correct order for the events. Number your paper from *1* to *5*. After the numbers write the underlined words from each sentence in the correct order. Then do the same for Part 2.

Part 1. Jacob decided to make himself some cereal.
First, he took out a bowl and spoon.
Then, he took the milk from the refrigerator and added some to his cereal.
Next, he took out a box of his favorite cereal and poured some of it into the bowl.
Finally, his tasty treat was ready.

Part 2. Shina and Peter bought their tickets at the ticket window.
With their boxes of popcorn, they entered the dark theater and found two seats.
They had a few minutes before the movie would begin, so they stopped in the lobby to buy popcorn.
Then a tall person sat in front of Peter.
"I can't see the screen," Peter whispered to Shina.

D. Expressing Yourself

Choose one of these activities.

1. Make up a story using some signal words such as *first, next, then, now, before, after, later, last,* and *finally.* As you write your story, leave blank lines where the signal words should go. Ask a classmate to fill in the signal words. Did your classmate fill in the same words that you would have used?
2. Write a story with one sentence out of order. Exchange stories with a classmate. Find the sentence that is out of order in each other's story, and figure out where the sentence belongs.